Stars of God
by
Presley L.B. Martin

Copyright © 2017 by Presley L.B. Martin

All rights reserved. This book or any portion thereof may not be reproduced or used in any manner whatsoever without the express written permission of the publisher except for the use of brief quotations in a book review.

Printed in the United States of America

First Printing, 2017
ISBN-10: 0-692-88841-1
ISBN-13: 978-0-692-88841-4

Photograph by Straub's Photography

Presley L.B. Martin

About the Author...

Presley L.B. Martin journeys this life in dreamscape forests by the lantern light of Moon and Sun. She creates art through writing, crocheting, drawing, painting, and crafting. But when she disengages from these activities, the realm of science fiction and fantasy governs her interests of film, game, and literature. Greater still, the science of astrology and the patterns of Nature revolve like the twelve stars 'round her Geminian mind.

Acknowledgements...

If it weren't for the memories of dancing Starlight, I doubt I would have caught any inspiration. And, in this life now, the smile and laughter of my little Sunshine mingling with that same Divinity solidifies my cause. Furthermore, the professionalism and aid of Alphagraphics-Evansville have fitted my artwork and writing into a stunning, dovetailed display, that of which I could only hope many months worth of self-effort would create. And last, but not least, I thank my husband for his sweet words of encouragement and his brilliant humor because, in this world, those closest to us truly make all the difference in our will, happiness, and success.

Forward

In infinite Darkness, the Womb stirs. His Mother wails as She labors, and the pain of the Falling Light becomes unbearable. Creation opens His sleepy eyes to the Dawning Light and knows what He must do. He Flies Forward into the Light, encompassed and in awe. Through His Mother's Womb and His Father's Seed, He became. Earth is His Body, the Ocean is His Blood, the Air is His Breath, the Life is His Warmth, and the Cosmic Spirit is His Soul. The First House is the Force that pushes the Sun Forward to His Birth. It is what most inspires the Entity to become His Sun, and to manifest His Will. This is His Ascendant.

In Further ado, this Age is Fathered by Lord Aquarius who has taken the First House as His Bride. Together, They produce a Sun whose Fate lies within Friendship and the eccentric Harmony to bind Creation under the Law of God. Troubles of a radical degree have materialized, and more are to be ensued, which have notoriously dubbed this Age as the Fabled "End of Times". In our World today, prophets are being born and demons are being made. The polar Scale of Good and Evil Flies high above like a Flag at noon peak. This Cosmic War is drafting all of Humanity for its cause. Lord Aquarius has decreed that none may escape and that all shall merge, or die in their slumber. "To be, or not to be" – to live or to fade away.

The Hearts of Men ring unto the World in desperate desire and pain. Their Subconscious Wisdom moves with the changing Universe, and they become afraid. But, in the Fire of God's Wrath, the iridescent Light may be seen. Like the Clouds who bring Rain for the Earth, the Aquarian Ascendant pours His beautiful, child-like Tears to nourish His Love For All. In astrological notation, an Aquarian Ascendant is the communal drive to harmonize or to disorganize the Creation of the perfect Heaven or the perfect Hell. In boundless dreams, revolution is everywhere.

This is the Force that directs our goals as one human consciousness. It is what unifies the human race, in which we, together, are destined to achieve a huge leap in our spiritual progress; thereupon, the Age of Aquarius awaits a cause for community.

We are given certain talents and desires to bring us together under one rule. However, not everyone has the same idea for a solitary rulership. On the far side of the sceptre, we see the most charitable and self-sacrificing of teachers. They devote their entire being to the service of humanity through Christ Consciousness by unification. The opposite of the sceptre contradicts everything that modern saints have worked towards. Total world domination and greed have transformed their chalice' water to putrid black ooze, bastardizing their own temple and creations. Between the extremes lies a wide array of grey to varying degrees, but the core of Aquarius remains the same. Now that Lord Aquarius governs the First House, we are obligated to unite, hand in hand, with our brothers and sisters.

As in the ancient, epic battle of the Sun kings, one king must take the other's place. Pisces, Lord of tradition, has liberated his mind by the wings of Death's hourglass. By the last fallen grain, our Merlin, Saturn, instructed his final lesson, and King Pisces perished. Thus, a new god-king has been appointed- one critical of the old ways and who demands a complete detoxification of the World Tree. His tears extract the hidden creatures from the dark recesses of the mind, preparing for war, for a revolution, for truth. In tribute to his coronation, Earth shall be harvested as a feast for the banquet where both heroes and lunatics dance and die.

Beginning in the early 20th century, the Age of Aquarius had begun. As a result, the Zodiac rides through the Heavens ascending with Aquarius, rather than our familiar Aries. The houses' skeleton remains strong, but hark that they have reestablished its lords. And, likewise, the widowed Seasons have taken new lovers. The natural cycle of birth, death, and rebirth doesn't end with Earth and Her children- the Heavens are just as much a part of that cycle as She. So now we must familiarize ourselves with the newborn Zodiac.

To ascertain that we are logically speaking with no tales of whimsical fancies, it is time to unwind the knots tied by modern, ego-centric stubbornness. Perhaps not all problems may be resolved by mathematics, but here it may prove a good teacher. Our solar system seems to travel at a different rate than common knowledge will have it. If you observe the Sky, you will notice that the Moon, the Sun, and the other planets are traveling at a pace that is approximately 60 degrees slower than what is reported by computers, the Farmers' Almanac, and current astronomy. According to my calculations based upon both my nightly observations and computer-generated, astrological reports, I have discovered a pattern and have found these following figures to be true:

Planet	Degree Rate per Month	Months and Years per Heavenly Revolution
Moon	360	1 Month
Venus	35	10 Months
Sun	30	1 Year
Mercury	30	1 Year
Mars	4	7 1/2 Years
Jupiter	2	15 Years
Saturn	2	15 Years
Uranus	1/2	60 Years
Neptune	1/4-1/3	90-120 Years
Pluto	1/4-1/3	90-120 Years

You yourself can determine this simply by calculating the degree difference every day for two months, and randomly selecting charts from a period of 20 years.

And now to verify that this information is correct, you must find these planets in the Sky and identify their positions in the constellations. This should be the same as in the online astrological charts, except that they are situated two signs before their current readings.

As to the nature of the houses, it, too, has undergone significant change. The definitions of the houses remain the same, but now they have acquired new environments. Rather than Aries representing the First House, it is Aquarius who carries on the responsibility. And you can see this pattern repeated with the remaining 11 houses.

But even with this bit of knowledge, the planets are their own selves and they will shift their movement in accordance with forces beyond Earth's realm for reasons beyond my Earthly mind.

Though you may believe standard astrology to accurately define your personality, it is only half true. It describes your personality very well, but only for the time of Aries, being the time of the biblical Moses. This age of information is in service of Aquarius.

But, before I explain their reign, I will dissertate the raw natures of these celestial divisions. Without the company of any lords, the houses are not always clearly defined. I have found that they follow patterns akin to the planetary aspects. These cosmic influences are shown below (for a better visual, see the house wheel at the end of this book).

1. The Manifestation of the Triumph of Spirit
2. The Unconscious Forces of the Triumph of Spirit
3. The Conscious Forces of the Triumph of Spirit
4. The Manifestation of the Triumph of Soul
5. The Unconscious Forces of the Triumph of Soul
6. The Conscious Forces of the Triumph of Soul
7. The Manifestation of the Triumph of Mental
8. The Unconscious Forces of the Triumph of Mental
9. The Conscious Forces of the Triumph of Mental
10. The Manifestation of the Triumph of Physical
11. The Unconscious Forces of the Triumph of Physical
12. The Conscious Forces of the Triumph of Physical

By understanding standard astrology (i.e. the houses having fixed rulers) and meditating upon celestial traffic, I am able to dissect their primal meanings.

As you gaze to the East, the Sun rises into the 12th house. From here it travels to the cusp of the 6th house as it approaches the Western horizon. It continues its course through the Night back to the 12th house of the Eastern horizon. This is one of the infinite portrayals of the life and death cycle. But why should we stop here? It is the key to understanding astrology! If you divide the Heavens into tripartite portions, you will have groups of four houses. Each group symbolizes a part of the cosmic cycle. From 12 to 9, the Sun experiences birth and childhood. In houses 8 to 5, old age progresses until Death. As it parts from its known body (i.e. the Day), the process of rebirth initiates from 4 till 1. And the cycle repeats. Alas! We must press on deeper into the ancient ruins if we wish to understand the complete Mystery.

As you may have already noticed, numerology plays a key role. If you divide the Sky into two dimensions, we see polarity- light versus dark, strength versus weakness, known versus unknown, conscious versus unconscious, good versus evil. If four quadrants are observed, we can relate this through the characteristics of the Seasons, the Winds, the Elements (with Spirit/Ether as the whole), and the suits of Tarot's Minor Arcana. If we manifest five divisions, the segments correspond with the five Elements, the Body's five extremities, and the five points of the Pentagram. By six, we can associate with the Hexagram (of the Star of David), the senses, and the balance of feminine and masculine. Seven-fold unveils the days of the week, the seven chakras, the colors of the rainbow, and the Heptagram (i.e. the Elven Star or the Eastern Star). Eight sections tells of the eight-spoked Wheel of the Year and Buddha's Eight-Fold Path. Nine separations can be linked to the nine realms of Heaven and Hell, Asatru's Nine-Fold Path, the nine Waves, the nine Muses, and the perfect trinity of three. Ten connects with the planets, and the Jewish and Christian Ten Commandments. Eleven finds the union of microcosm and macrocosm and the imbalanced polarity of Yin and Yang. Lastly, twelve identifies with the twelve evolved chakras, the months of the year, and the word analogies of the Zodiac (i.e. "I Feel", "I am", "I think", etc.).

Along with numerological patterns, one must also be able to correctly identify the phases of the Sun. We have Dawn, Waxing Sun, Noon Peak, Waning Sun, and Dusk. However, Night should be of equal consideration. After Sunset, the Sky is dark, and will continue to become darker until it reaches true Twilight. This is the darkest hour and will vary, depending on the time of the year. From here, the Sun begins its true Waxing phase until Noon Peak. Dawn is simply the observable Waxing Sun, whereas Dusk is the observable Waning Sun.

Accompanying the other planets, a very important lesson may be conceived. The cosmic bodies do not follow a schedule, but rather a schedule follows the cosmic bodies. It is folly to believe that for more than a hundred years, twilight occurs at precisely 12 am. This may have been the case at certain intervals, but when the Sun travels at an approximate speed of 30 degrees each month of approximately 30 days, Greenwich Standard Time must consistently rewrite herself new schedules.

Nothing in Nature conforms to a "cookie-cutter" pattern. With that said, astrological computer programs must also continuously update their charts.

> The Heavens revolve around the North Star, Polaris, whom Ursa Major, or the Big Dipper, closely circumnavigates. During the Vernal Equinox, the "pot" part of the Big Dipper mounts on top of its "handle". In Native American lore, the "pot" is referred to as the Great Bear who battles the three Hunters (the "handle") from blossom to harvest and returned.

To begin any configuration of an astrological chart, one must be sure that he or she is working with the correct time of the year. This component dictates the Sun's condition which will alter the planetary placements in the houses by 4 to 5 hours. Correspondingly, if the Hunters are seated atop the constellation, Ursa Major has been slain and the Autumnal Equinox has begun. However, in Winter, the Bear endures death and rebirth and faces left. In the heat of Summer, the trail is hot on the Bear who runs from the Hunters to the right. The months may be found by estimating the degrees of its turn from equinox to solstice, and solstice to equinox. This is a very accurate approach, especially considering there is only a three month difference between the events. But you must understand, too, that our King, Ursa Major, will chase and flee from the hunters throughout the Cosmos. At times, he may be cozily close to Draco, yet, at another time will reside as far as Hydra's domain, while every celestial body including itself will forever continue their revolution around the North Star.

The Big Dipper seems to obey only its own orbit. Likewise, the Zodiac Wheel (Ecliptic) will vary its flight throughout the year, and will travel from left to right as you gaze South from the Northern Hemisphere. From about March till June, the Wheel will seem to "engulf" the Southern Sky. As the year progresses, it will gradually turn. During the Vernal Equinox, the Wheel honors the Southern Sky. At Midsummer, it takes homage in the West. As the Autumnal Equinox approaches, it pays tribute to the North. At last, it will rest in the East for Midwinter.

While it is essential to know and to observe these patterns, one's own psychic intuition will be the true guide to reading the Universe. As stated earlier, Nature is far from anything absolute. There is really no convenience in monitoring the numbers and calculations other than for the mental, intellectual security of our out-of-tuned personalities.

> In the East, we have the Ascendant whose purpose is to provide its life force to nurture the life of the Sun. In the same manner, the chariot that guides the Heavens is similar to the Ascendant, driving the very life of the Cosmos.

We must now consider the environment in which the Universe thrives. How do we truly know what something is if we only understand its mechanisms and not its body? What dimensions form it? Originally, all abided by geocentricity until, in 1531, Nicolaus Copernicus presented the World with the heliocentric model. The scientific community took this idea by its reigns and forcefully drove it into the heads of modern civilization. In my opinion, the questions of its origins, purpose, and validity must be satisfied before it should be fully integrated into astrology.

Before we can go any further, we must completely disregard the notion that everything taught to us is absolute truth. We are taught to depend on the facts and to ignore our imagination and intuition. But what if these facts are lies? Does this make our perception of reality a lie as well? Let you and your intuition be the judges. Though I am no witness to the Realm of the Gods Above, I have great suspicion of the heliocentric concept. Because of its great popularity and utter aggressiveness against any who dare to defy it, a logical person should suspect a deception, for countless of times history has proven this to us through patterns. As the saying goes "history always repeats itself".

Though I do not deny their genius and sincerity, almost every popular astrological source obtains their information from computer programs and NASA-oriented organizations engineered to deceive the masses. The closer you are to a lie, the more intense the friction between good and evil becomes, spiritually being the same wavelength of nails scratching down a chalkboard. But, the more you reckon with truth, the greater the expansion of your soul shall be. If you relate this psychology with the situation, a clearer perception will emerge.

> There are other books that provide a detailed explanation of Copernicus, the Jesuits, the Catholic Church, and their histories, but here I place my emphasis on the "Naturally Psychic World".

Geocentricity (otherwise known as the Flat Earth Theory) is quite agreeable with astrology because it creates a simplified structure that follows the same rhythm as the rest of Nature. The mere closeness of the Gods' Realm with our own world builds a proportionately intimate relationship with the Divine, compared to the untimely distance of Outer Space. It is another attempt to separate the Creator from humanity, and we are fools for blindly accepting an ideology without doing our homework. Question the authority of Man's instructions!

I am merciful, and I do understand mistakes, but the information that I have read on several well-known and reputable astronomical websites has disturbed me. Though it may seem like a minuscule issue to argue, it is something that every professional astronomer should, without excuse, correctly identify. Their daily and monthly charts demonstrate the Sun, the Moon, and the remaining planets as repeatedly being positioned two signs ahead of current times. So, in other words, if the Moon in the Sky is in Leo, these sources will portray it as in Libra. How do I conclude this? By turning my eyes away from the computer screen and to let them rest evenly upon the Heavenly Lights as Nature intended!

In a similar scenario, rumor has further pushed the claim that Ophiuchus (the Serpent Bearer) is the 13th constellation. Again, the Sky does not lie. Ophiuchus is situated roughly above Scorpio and does not lie within the Ecliptic. It remains just as distant from Scorpio as Lepus is from Libra. Therefore, the Serpent Bearer has no rank within the Zodiac Kingdom.

In as much, the Zodiac Wheel does not deviate from ancient lore. Has the wisdom of the Ages not taught that change is inevitable? When it is Winter, it does not remain Winter. It grows into Spring; Spring into Summer; Summer into Autumn; and Autumn back into Winter. Similarly, there was a time called Aries, and after came Pisces. Presently, King Aquarius sits upon the Heavenly Throne and, by his rule, astrology has evolved. But remember, too, that life does not end with him and nor does it end with any other Zodiac Lord. And like every other Zodiac Lord, Aquarius has a story, and we must elope on its adventures to conceive its Magic and Mysteries.

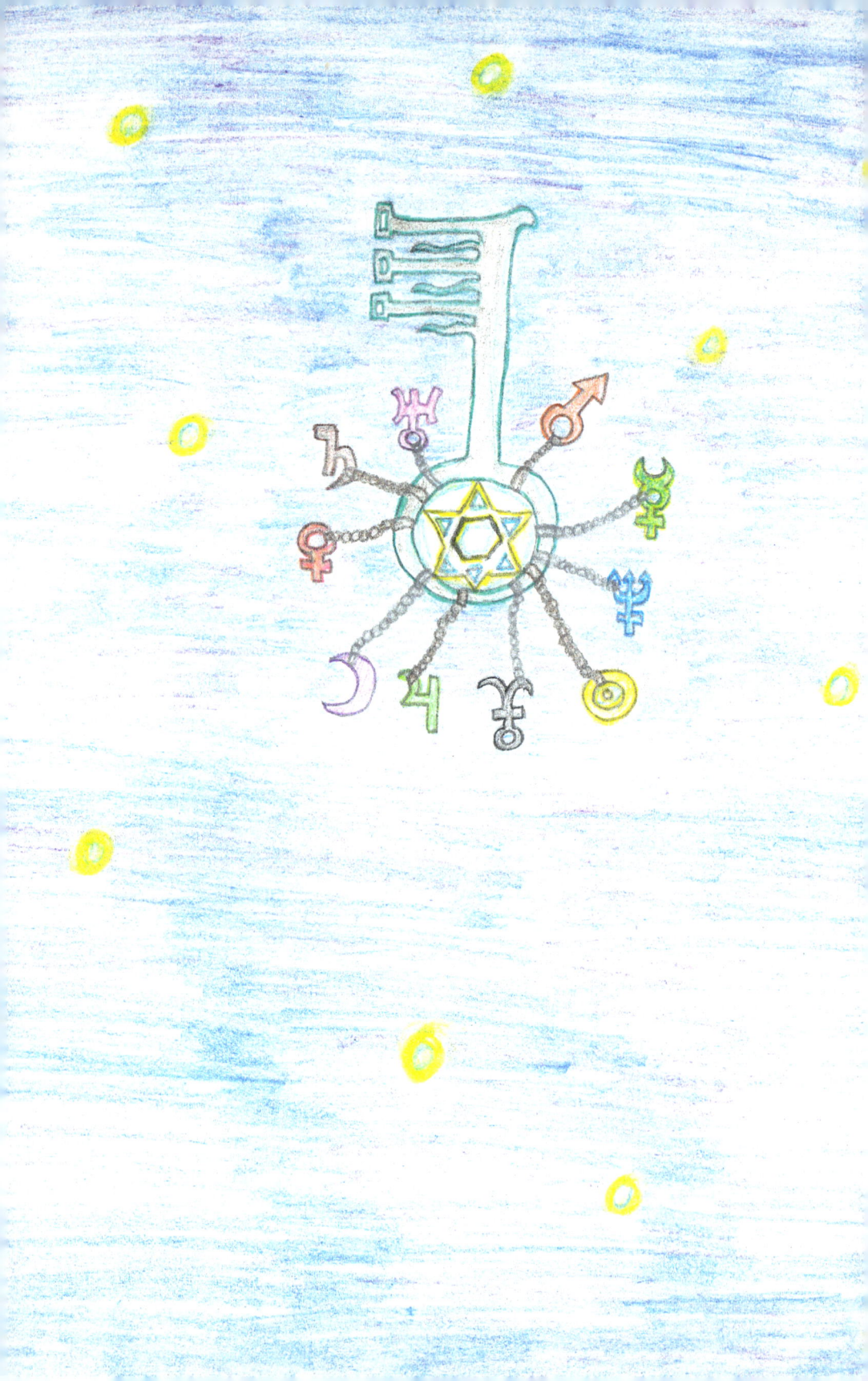

First House Ruled by Aquarius...
The Revolutionary Kingdom

An electric Storm exhales,
In heavy Dew Collect,
Through the Eyes who perceive,
The Power of Reality.

Upon the Charge of Rain,
The heavenly Steed thunders to Life,
Static Pollen flying off Its galloping Hooves.

Follow Its Tail,
And You will surely glide to the Dragon's Head,
Whose Wings beat betwixt Balance,
Falling and rising like the North and South Winds.

Behind the Chaos,
Behold the Eye of the Storm!
A Cloud calmed as a Throne,
Fashioned for the Floating Crown.
      Omnipresent Song sung,
To the Sequence of a Sword sharpened.

Down the Throat of the World,
You will see,
A Sky drunk deep of living Water,
Fixed from the Holy Grail.

Second House Ruled by Pisces...
The High-Priestess of Avalon

Lore Tide cradles the Ocean Spring,
To Autumn, to Winter, and back again.

Stays to sing,
The Sea-Maid listens and Her heart is won,
The love of Life,
Her Sea-King.

Blue in Depths,
Sailing the Shades,
River Mouth pours the Ocean,
By the Moonlight of Moonset.

Scaled with Tributaries,
Engraved into the Land,
Knowing Its Course,
Despite the Shifting Sand.

Following a Thought,
Taught from Mother,
Learned in good Faith,
A Symphony of Grace.

Knowledge is Power,
Every Formula in Memory,
You can swim anywhere,
That the Ocean yields.

Nestled in Study upon the Sea Bed,
Collect Your Knowledge from all the Quarters,
And unite in Whole the Creature of the Species.

A Cell will be Dark,
If no Light will bind,
From Its Walls and out.
Thus a Mansion You shall truly find,
When the Light seals every Imperfection,
And creates Life within the Womb.

Third House Ruled by Aries...
The Fire in the Sky

In the Night a Mountain stirs,
Boulders colliding with Stagnation.

Upon my Horns the Sun does rise,
Hewn from Ruby Embers.

In Chase we think the Sun does flee,
Unrelenting through Moonshadow Fall.

Still the Heart strives Freely,
Laughing as Children at play.

Ought the Hoof to tremble or stumble,
Not a Wink of Fear,
not a Tear of Despair.

A Fire Flies into the Night,
With Day upon his Shoulders,
And casts away the Shadows,
Who dare to disrupt his beautiful Dream.

The Bengal Tiger on the Prowl,
Howl like the Vigilante Wolf.

A Hero indeed for promising Justice,
Pondering in Love Lore Whispers.

Prance to the Day's End,
Heart throbbing with whistling Hymns.

Heed of Song for the merry Young of Earth,
To the Sun who shines bright in Heaven,

Beyond any Mountain Noon,
Within a Story,
Even surpassing the Moon.

I am the Light of the Universe,
My Fire burns hotly,
Upon the Coals of My Core.

I am made into the Pyre that,
Consecrates the Death of ancient Heroes.
I am the Flame that penetrates the Darkness,
Uniting the Sword with Her Knight,
The Scholar with His Quill,
The Mage with His Wand,
The Sceptre with Her King.

I am a Child at Play,
The Inner Light wizened beyond Time.

The Animals understand Me, and I Them,
My Garden is My Jungle,
And My Jungle is My Garden.

Innocence is the River of Life,
Where I drink, bathe, and travel upon.

Where Love is Found, I am there,
Where I am, Love is Found.

4th House ruled by Taurus...
The Cosmic Courtyard

To the Genesis of the Earth,
From the Stars who sing above the Sun,
The misty Land awakes,
To the thundering Oxen quakes.

The Love who I dance to,
The spiraling Song of Nature.

I am here as Your Knight,
In solemn Loyalty Forevermore.

I will guard Your Fortress,
And the Crown which animates You.

Wild Beasts roar and grunt,
I am the Hunter who knows every Tongue.

Twinkling Eyes wander in the Night,
I am the Priest who guides Your Gaze to the Light.

I am Your Mother and I am Your Father,
Your Lover and Your Friend.

Yonder there o'er the stormy Sea,
A Lighthouse beaconing in Peace.

Foreign Ships sail to Her Heart,
Desperate against the bull rut Rocks.
Shipwrecks abound,
Drowning to Their underwater Graves.

The Ox looks out across the Sea,

As the Sea looks back to His shining Eye.

In Forgotten Lands, strong and old,
It is still the Stronghold,
Of elvish Wit and mannish Lore.

Here they long reside as Custom,
As Custom besits in rural Craftsmanship.

Honor adorns Their Brow,
So they see fit the Forests to the Land.

But the Plants to the Rocks,
To the Spirits of Hole and Cavern,
In Earth Their Prowess is honed,
The ancient Dwarves who pray to the Heartgem,
Bejeweled by Divine Grace.

From Dreams Eon,
Soil and Breath do turn,
To Fruit for Children evermore.

The Cow who blesses Her Young,
With Life and Home,
The Rain who pours for the Fruits,
Flock to the Shepherd who teaches Peace,
The Prince of Peace and His Princess Bride.

5th House ruled by Gemini...
The Alchemy of Karma

The North Watchtower oversees Her Tribes,
Her Children are Her Glory,
Singing in the Wind,
Breathing Life into and from the Love of Their kind Voices.

The Ice is warm and the Leaves are green,
She is the Wizard's Abode of the highest Dream.

Hospitality is Her Refuge,
The generous Peasant dwells,
On Her richest Estate.

A Song of Years foretells,
Joy and Sorrow forever after.

The musical Egg of Ruby and Sapphire,
Emerald, Copper, and Gold,
Courts the Heartbeat of Love's Mist,
In the Night's Ballet.

The Twin of the North has flown South,
With the Birds and the Fish to warm Climes.

In strange Kin She is merry,
But the Fruit of Her Village rejoices in the same Tongue.

True to Her Name and true to the Light,
Which nourishes the Earth,
From Infinity ago to Infinity ahead,
Hand in Hand She walks with Her Twin,
From East to West to East again,
The holy Path of the starry Spirit.

6th House ruled by Cancer...
The Rippling Waters of the Cauldron

In soft blue Dreams I swim with Glee,
Onto the Shores of the Dusk's Lagoon.

Bewildering Fancies and bubbling Toasts,
Hearken the shining Moon's Light,
The Heaven's innocent Host.

I am calling from My Heart,
To My Mind insane,
A Plea for Understanding,
And Rejoice in Music ancient and Fair.

In awe I gaze up to My Mother and Father,
Encompassed in a Blanket of nursing Serenity.
A crystal Palace wrought with Iridescence,
Inside, the Princess with white, pearly Locks,
In aural Gown,
Spinning and Dancing in childlike Trance.

Her Spirit is Free,
Abound with twelve Stars in All,
The Tiara She wears is a Token from,
The Bounty of Her Dreams come true.

In the Bosom of the Sea,
There I lay,
The Eggs of Creation,
Bounty of Home.
A Pearl for One is a Pearl for All,
Blessing the Dove,
Who doth share a Tale,
Of peaceful Union.

7th House Ruled by Leo...
The King of Dancing Swords

At the Fireside stands He at the Mantle,
The Mantle of the Hearth of His Father's Home.

He sees into the Face of the Woodland,
Laughing and Frolicking,
In warm motherly Love.

This is who He is,
He is at Peace,
Nestled in Honor that upholds,
Life on Its Shoulders.

Happiness overflows like a Fountain of Gold,
More than all Tithe From,
The Temple's Excellence.

A proud Father makes a proud Son,
The King who cries in nostalgic Joy,
For the Love of His Kingdom and Her Peoples.

He remembers the Sundance,
Thinking on a Midsummer's Dream,
And those Things He has put,
His Life into creating,
Is finally prepared for the Holiday,
Of the Autumn Harvest Day.

From a Page fumbling with His Sword,
To a King of an unbreakable Wield,
His highest Conquest lies,
In Balance between His Mind and His Heart.

A perfect Figure the Lion ponders,
In swept the Wind clutching hold,
The Lampstand Fire.

With Strength I will make Your Pyre cold,
With Strength I smelt into golden Wisdom,
The Light of the Sky.

Stay warm by My Side,
I will hold You as a Son.
          Like My Eyes gaze above,
Bells ringing in Hand and Ear,
To the Celebration of the Age.

Cast from the Paw,
Blazing Torrents bravely,
I am the Seeker who knows All.

A Tooth fights with dying Victory,
But Centuries past,
The Flame of My Lamp,
Remains ever alight,
By Her Sentry Courage.

A thousand Swords,
My Roar has pierced,
The Riddles of Antiquity.

Snowflake Petals ring 'round My Head,
Eyes alone cannot hold Me,
For the only Master is I,
I the shining Holiness.

8th House Ruled by Virgo...
The Maiden Behind the Veil

Upon the Earth I have lived,
Under sway of Moon.

Every Dream I have held,
To My Heart so dear,
I have blessed in Design,
A World of Caves and of Forests,
A World of Ocean and of Mystery,
A World untold of Legends lost,
To be Found in Works of Heroes,
Adventurers abound in Depths unfathomed,
The bardic Language sung in Nature.

Under Heaven I am owed,
All Woes to My Care,
Like My Mother and Hers before Her.

A Harp of Gold twines Millenia,
In Thyme Couplets laid to My Spring,
Follow the Dove to this Water,
And there Ye will find,
Your Temple 'dorned,
In Flora Cornucopia.

Over yonder a golden Castle sits,
Solemn as the Cemetery Winds.

The Face who haunts the Wanderer,
That drifted into the Mists.

Over in yore lost Tales may be Found,
Over Pages spilled by undying Ink.

In the Grey-Haven,
A Knight slumbers in Wait,
The motionless Stag rivals this uncanny.

The ceaseless Salmon who returns,
After the River's End,
Will listen to this Secret.

Ordinary arms will not encircle,
An Honor as pure.

The Knight opens His Eyes,
And the Fog divides before Him,
Onwards He goes to the Castle Golem.

As a chaste Virgin,
The Fortress of Stone,
Is a precious Jewel at Heart.

Her Keepers are the Saints of Time,
Donned in Robes of white and red,
And they have heard the Proclamation,
Of the Knight's Pilgrimage.

A warm Toast with Goblets of spiced Wine,
To salute His Arrival,
In Courtesy He acknowledges,
Their Greetings with the Gift,
Of His only Helm and Sword.

Her Majesty approaches,
Laying Her Hand onto His downcast Head,

At Pray before the Altar.

Her Light is like to none Other,
The Angels of High Heaven,
Hail by Song and Lyre,
Voices dressed in Choir.

They as Two climb the spiraling Stairs,
To the Height of the Tower of Golem Castle.

The Door is pushed open to the World,
Where Day never grows old,
And the Birds sing in Ensemble,
To Eden, to Avalon,
Behind the misty Vale.

And so is the Dream-Tale of Sir Galahad and His virgin Bride.

9th House Ruled by Libra...
The Village Elder

Stars of God

The Day is hot,
In Flight o'er,
Her Heartstrings light taught.

A Harp of gentle Breeze,
Its Aroma sweet and Fair,
To the All-Smelling Nostrils,
Below the Eye who ever stares,
From the Face of Justice,
From a Lord humble and patient.

The Merchants share Gold,
The Law counts Blessings,
I look to the Lady with Hands of Pearl,
Outstretched from Arms of Jewels.

The Day is Tropic,
On Her crystalline Body,
Breathing as Sunlight in Trot.

All who take Refuge at Her Court,
Dance with open Arms,
As do the Great-Horned Owls that Fly.

Her City hums in auric Liberty,
By the Generator of Light,
In Bonds of Love bound.

The Spirit in judicial Violet,
 Plucks a Feather,
From the Wings of the hallowed Staff,
To take up the Quill,

And write divine Order,
And to uphold Harmony,
The holy Bard of the Temple's Crown.

Upon the Dove's Brow,
The Star of Liberty honors the Light,
As a Beacon of Friendship ,
To Land and Ocean,
By both Day and Night.

In the Eye of Pendragon,
A Sword and Shield beheld,
Worn amongst the sunnied Helm,
Below the starlit Brim,
Showers of Lilies,
Salute the Judge,
In hallowed Halls,
Courting His Queen of Peace.

'Twain the Flag and the Stone,
My serene Heart lays before the Lamb.

As a Priest Familiar high and low,
Robed in grey,
And cloaked in brilliant Lantern Light,
Hailed by the Sword in Stone,
I voyage yonder Meadows,
To Hermitage exhalt.

Pull close to the Brain,
Witness Your Sight,
The Wit lain as a Cloth,
Upon the Altar's highest,
As the Crow Flies.

10th House Ruled by Scorpio...
The Naked Roots of the Ash

Hearken a Tale dipped from the Well,
Told of Wisdom and Longings whispered,
'Round the Shoulders who uphold,
The World of both Good and Evil.

Leaves grow curiously,
Falling mysteriously,
Appearing again in paradoxical Madness.

Philosophers meditate upon Her Stone,
In perfect Spirit in the Pool of Waters,
Who ever live.

Rippling in Choir a Melody higher,
The Spirit who inquires Destiny's Desire.

God-Wind brewed in ethereal Light,
Penetrates the Ocean's darkest Depths,
Cleansing the Vessel,
And Restoring the Spring of Youth.

She is the Maiden who loves Her Garden,
For what It is and what It isn't.

She is the brilliant Child,
Knowing the Arts of Sciences,
And the Sciences of Arts,
Delving into the World unexplored,
Adventuring the Garden's Infinite.

In love I hold the Tears,
Possessed by the Vase,

Who Fruits a Bouquet,
Of both withering and blooming Flowers.

The Doctrines by the Sages of yore,
Followed by light Frolicking Footsteps,
Plants Islands in the Sea,
And drowns the rocky Barrens,
As sudden with Purpose,
As the twinkling Stars in Heaven.

In Time You will witness,
My Endeavors to gracefully unfold,
At Times in the bleak Cold,
You will relate to My Powers,
By the Force or the Desire,
You exert into the World.

I am the Sword who has made Men into Kings,
The Excalibur who shines Brilliance,
Enraptured by His right Hand's Wield.

The Truth I share,
Is a Treasure greater than Its Chest,
An endless Chalice of living Water,
Gifted to My People.

In Revelations enlightened,
I am the Sign of Your Savior,
The Hope that transcends Life from Death.

Let the Tides be,
And the Fish swim Free,

Weave Your Net in gossamer Faith,
And Cast it open to the Sunlight,
For as You gaze across the Sea,
You will see My Light,
Dance before the Tidings.

11th House Ruled by Sagittarius...
The Pyramid in the Earth

Under the Mountain I sleep as the Bear,
As a Blanket of white envelops My Cradle.

The Dwarves of Subterra clash Their Hammers,
Skillfully striking the Anvil,
In unyielding Fury.

Let the Animals who burrow,
Arise at Spring beneath,
And throw the Hell to the Wolves,
With gnashing Teeth.

My Heart burns wildly,
By the Bellows of My Forge,
I feed Her My Enchanted Metals,
And all of My Father's Craft,
For the Bounty of Love,
Greater than the Palace of My Ancestors.

I have perfected My Designs,
Technology impeccable,
To extract My Final Creation,
Of which only Me and these Caves know.

Consider My Work to be done,
When My Bones become stubborn,
And My Tools in Decay,
For that is what My Assurance will afford.
But My Rest lies awake,
For the Death of another Century,
And until then will My Rest,
Only be in Peace.

Below My Snowy Mountain,
Within the Chambers of My Forge.

The Handle who chases the Bear,
In Hunt For His Life,
The Boundary Finely kept,
To maintain stable Law.

As the World is in my Custody,
I am Her Ego behind Forgotten Powers,
Protector of secret Vaults,
Releasing Her Knowledge,
With Bow drawn to Cheek,
As She gradually matures,
Blossoming as divinely decreed.

In My Library You will discover,
A Realm of magical Wisdom,
Adventure inlaid with hidden Manna,
Within the Confines,
Of the Bookshelf Door,
And the Great-Horned Owl at Its Foot.

12th House Ruled by Capricorn...
The Sacrificed Lamb

In the gladdened Forest,
The Wood Elves do live,
Amongst the ancient Oaks,
And Her Fauna at Play,
Under a Sky clad in green Leaves.

Before Them at Their Kingdom Hall,
They set the dining Table,
With the Fruits of Their Labor,
Laid 'round a simple Cornucopia.

A greedy Man would think of this,
And none else,
A wise Man perceives,
The Nature of His World,
And shares His Table with It.

Children know the Key,
To every Corner and Crevice,
As a Torch enables Sight,
Within the Darkness.

The Seasons must change,
The Wind blows on,
The Nine Waves ebb and Flow,
And so must We.

A Heart of Gold is worth more than It mined,
The Wood Elves gather Their Harvest,

To nourish the gladdened Forest,
And the Spirits of Her Creatures.

The Artist who riddles,
In innocent Beauty,
Invites the Holy Spirit,
Into His Home.

The Stars She had cast,
Her greatest Wish upon,
Are falling quickly,
To Earth, Sea, and Sky.

Shoots of Life unfold Their Leaves,
Uncurling cosmic Mystery,
In Mountain Folds,
Of dawning Spring Essence.

Before the Kingdom,
And Eras of Prosperity,
Here only chaste Existence,
Inhabits Our Dimension,
Taking only what You need from It.

Breath and Body collide in Union,
And a Way is made,
Through Tunnel kaleidoscopic,
Into the Light,
As Our Lord,
Rains in euphoric Tears.

House 1
House 2
House 3
House 4
House 5
House 6
House 7
House 8
House 9
House 10
House 11
House 12

www.ingramcontent.com/pod-product-compliance
Lightning Source LLC
Chambersburg PA
CBHW042335150426
43194CB00005B/165